YELLOWSTONE

A REDISCOVERY

EDWARD TYLER

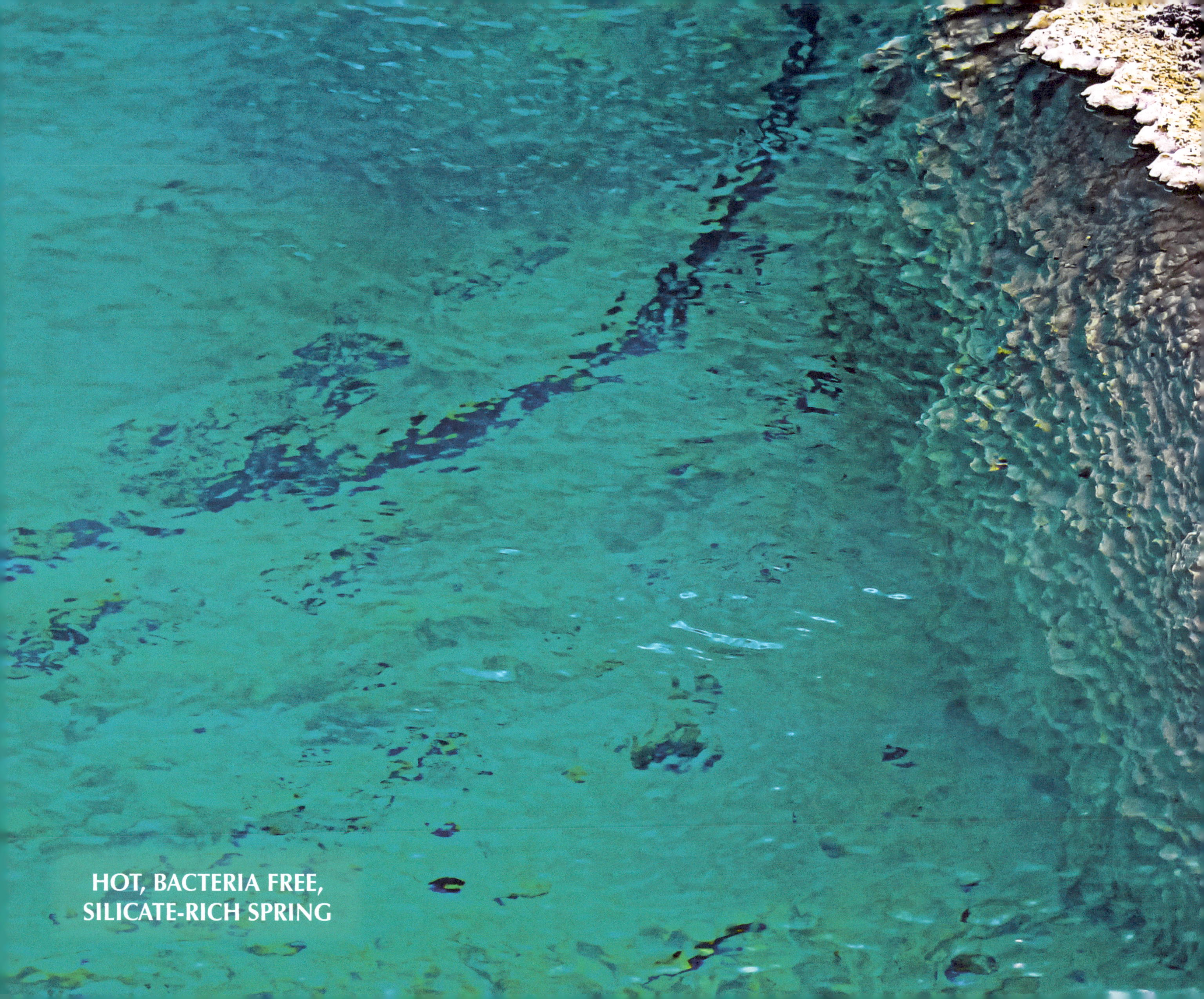
HOT, BACTERIA FREE,
SILICATE-RICH SPRING

COVER DESIGN AND PHOTOGRAPHS

EDWARD TYLER

TEXT AND INTERIOR PHOTOGRAPHS

EDWARD TYLER

FORNAX ADVENTURE

Mission - Explore less frequented regions, inspire others towards adventure, and encourage a profound appreciation and stewardship of Earth, our home in the cosmos.

Fornax is a seemingly unremarkable constellation in the southern hemisphere. During 2003 and 2004 the Hubble Telescope was pointed into the seemingly black space within this constellation. After completing an exposure equivalent to eleven days, an image known as the Hubble Ultra Deep Field was produced. This image revealed nearly 10,000 galaxies in otherwise black space. Exploration into the uknown beyond the horizon is the spirit behind Fornax Adventure.

Thanks to Christopher and Heather for inspiring others to appreciate Montana for its big skies and natural wonders.

Special thanks to my parents for their love and support over the years.

REFERENCES:

Map of Yellowstone National Park on page vii produced by the National Park Service (NPS). Public domain. No claim to original U.S. Government works. Map is NOT intended for back country hiking, water navigation, mountaineering, and other specialized activities. Use United States Geological Survey (USGS) topographic maps instead.

Page 63. Image of Kiowa. By BPL - In Summer, Kiowa Uploaded by Fæ, CC BY 2.0, https://commons.wikimedia.org/w/index.php?curid=15935236. No changes.

Montana State University, 2013. *Living Colors: Microbes of Yellowstone National Park*. Thermal Biology Institute.

Reference or inclusion does not constitute endorsement of the material in this book.

Other books by Edward Tyler:
"Antarctica: Tales of the Explorers"
"Glacier National Park: A Rediscovery"
"Our Place, Time, and Purpose in the Cosmos"

MONTANA / WYOMING

Cooke City is open all year

Northeast Entrance 7365 ft 2245 m
Northeast Entr to Red Lodge
212

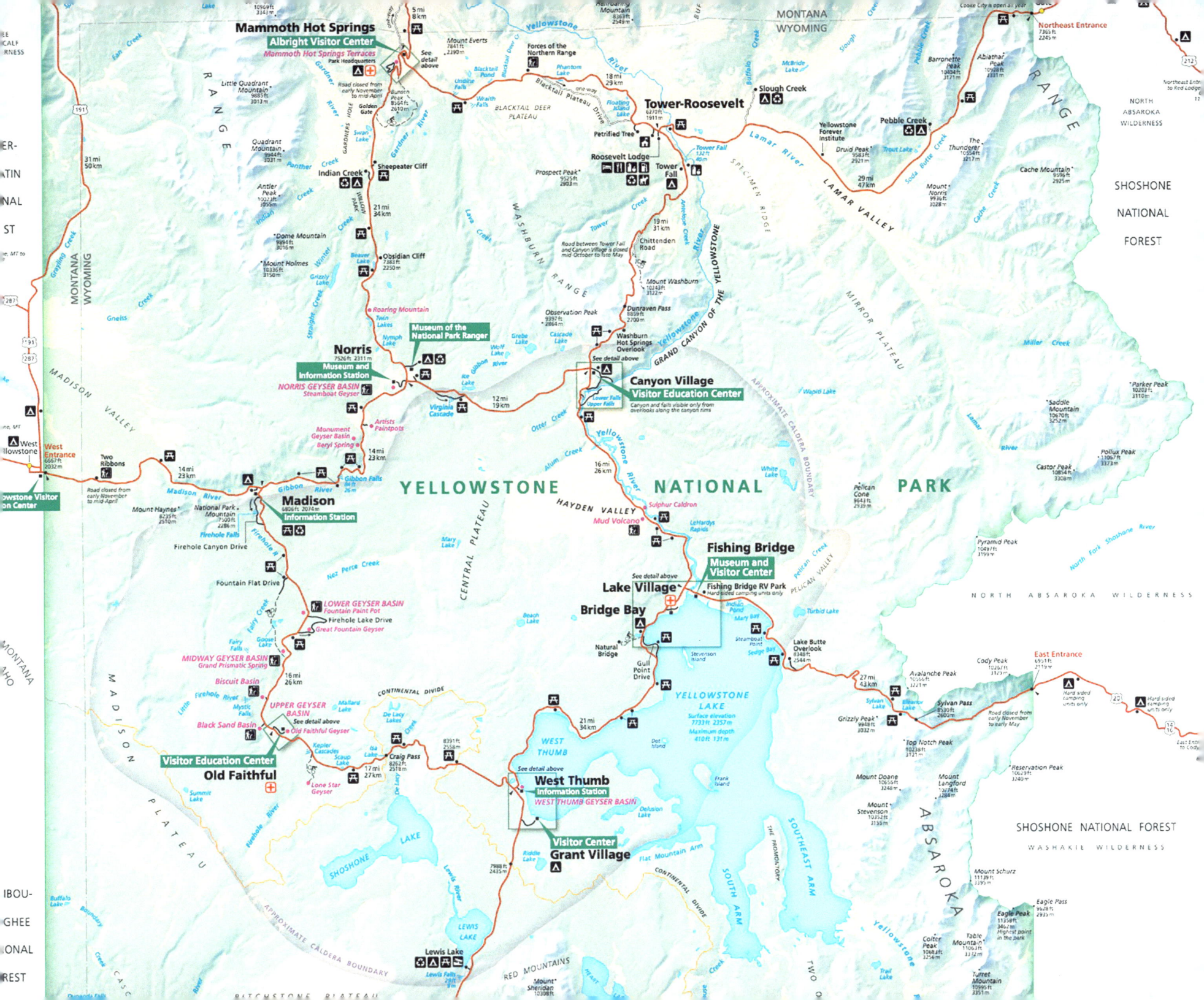

Mammoth Hot Springs
Albright Visitor Center
Mammoth Hot Springs Terraces
Park Headquarters
See detail above

Mount Everts 7841 ft 2390 m
Forces of the Northern Range
Yellowstone River
5 mi / 8 km
18 mi / 29 km

Little Quadrant Mountain 9885 ft 3013 m
Gardiner River
Undine Falls
Wraith Falls
Blacktail Pond
Phantom Lake
BLACKTAIL DEER PLATEAU
Blacktail Plateau Drive — one-way

Tower-Roosevelt 6270 ft 1911 m
Slough Creek
Yellowstone Forever Institute
Petrified Tree
Roosevelt Lodge
Tower Fall 132 ft 40 m
Druid Peak 9583 ft 2921 m
Trout Lake
Pebble Creek
McBride Lake
Barronette Peak 10404 ft 3171 m
Abiathar Peak 10928 ft 3331 m
The Thunderer 10554 ft 3217 m
Cache Mountain 9966 ft 3028 m

NORTH ABSAROKA WILDERNESS

191 / MONTANA WYOMING

Quadrant Mountain 10216 ft 3111 m
Antler Peak 10023 ft 3055 m
Indian Creek
Sheepeater Cliff
Golden Gate
Bunsen Peak 8564 ft 2610 m
Prospect Peak 9525 ft 2903 m
Tower Fall
29 mi / 47 km
19 mi / 31 km

GARDNERS HOLE
WILLOW PARK
21 mi / 34 km

LAMAR River
LAMAR VALLEY
SPECIMEN RIDGE
WASHBURN RANGE
Lava Creek
Tower Creek

Mount Norris 9936 ft 3028 m

SHOSHONE NATIONAL FOREST

31 mi / 50 km
ER-TIN NAL ST
Panther Creek
Indian Creek
Winter Creek
Straight Creek

Dome Mountain 9894 ft 3016 m
Mount Holmes 10336 ft 3150 m
Beaver Lake
Obsidian Cliff 7383 ft 2250 m
Grizzly Lake
Roaring Mountain
Twin Lakes
Nymph Lake

Chittenden Road
Mount Washburn 10243 ft 3122 m
Road between Tower Fall and Canyon Village is closed mid-October to late May

Museum of the National Park Ranger

Observation Peak 9397 ft 2864 m
Dunraven Pass 8859 ft 2700 m
Washburn Hot Springs Overlook
Grebe Lake
Cascade Lake
Wolf Lake
Ice Lake
See detail above

GRAND CANYON OF THE YELLOWSTONE
MIRROR PLATEAU
Miller Creek
Parker Peak 10203 ft 3110 m

Norris
7526 ft 2311 m
Museum and Information Station
NORRIS GEYSER BASIN
Steamboat Geyser

Canyon Village
Visitor Education Center
Lower Falls
Upper Falls
Canyon and falls visible only from overlooks along the canyon rims

Virginia Cascade
Artists Paintpots
Monument Geyser Basin
Beryl Spring
12 mi / 19 km
14 mi / 23 km

Otter Creek
Re Lake Drop
Saddle Mountain 10670 ft 3252 m
Lamar River
Wapiti Lake

MADISON VALLEY
Gneiss Creek

191 / 287
287

West Entrance 6667 ft 2032 m
Yellowstone Visitor Center
Two Ribbons
Road closed from early November to mid-April

14 mi / 23 km
Madison River
Gibbon River
Gibbon Falls 84 ft 25 m

Madison
6806 ft 2074 m
Information Station
National Park Mountain 7500 ft 2286 m
Mount Haynes 8235 ft 2510 m
Firehole Falls
Firehole Canyon Drive

YELLOWSTONE   **NATIONAL**   **PARK**

CENTRAL PLATEAU
Mary Lake
HAYDEN VALLEY
Sulphur Caldron
Mud Volcano
LeHardys Rapids
16 mi / 26 km

Fishing Bridge
Museum and Visitor Center
Lake Village
Bridge Bay
Fishing Bridge RV Park
Hard-sided camping units only
Indian Pond
Mary Bay
White Lake
Turbid Lake
Pelican Creek
PELICAN VALLEY
Pelican Cone 9643 ft 2939 m
Pyramid Peak 10049 ft 3199 m

NORTH ABSAROKA WILDERNESS

Fountain Flat Drive
Nez Perce Creek
LOWER GEYSER BASIN
Fountain Paint Pot
Firehole Lake Drive
Great Fountain Geyser
Fairy Falls
Goose Lake
MIDWAY GEYSER BASIN
Grand Prismatic Spring
Biscuit Basin
Firehole River
Mystic Falls
16 mi / 26 km

UPPER GEYSER BASIN
See detail above
Black Sand Basin
Old Faithful Geyser

Mallard Lake
CONTINENTAL DIVIDE
De Lacy Lakes
De Lacy Creek

Natural Bridge
Gull Point Drive
Steamboat Point
Sedge Bay
Lake Butte Overlook 8348 ft 2544 m

YELLOWSTONE LAKE
Surface elevation 7733 ft 2357 m
Maximum depth 410 ft 131 m
Stevenson Island
Beach Lake

East Entrance 6951 ft 2119 m
Avalanche Peak 10566 ft 3221 m
Cody Peak 10267 ft 3129 m
27 mi / 43 km
Sylvan Lake
Eleanor Lake
Sylvan Pass
Road closed from early November to early May
Hard-sided camping units only
Grizzly Peak 9948 ft 3032 m
Top Notch Peak 10238 ft 3121 m
East Entr to Cody
20 / 14 / 16

Mount Doane 10656 ft 3248 m
Mount Langford 10774 ft 3284 m
Mount Stevenson 10352 ft 3155 m

Old Faithful
Visitor Education Center
Summit Lake
Lone Star Geyser
Kepler Cascades
Scaup Lake
Craig Pass 8262 ft 2518 m
Isa Lake
8391 ft 2558 m
17 mi / 27 km

West Thumb
Information Station
WEST THUMB GEYSER BASIN
See detail above
Delusion Lake
Frank Island
WEST THUMB
21 mi / 34 km
Dot Island

Grant Village
Visitor Center
Riddle Lake
Flat Mountain Arm

THE PROMONTORY
SOUTHEAST ARM
SOUTH ARM

Mount Schurz 11139 ft 3395 m
RED MOUNTAINS
Mount Sheridan 10308 ft 3141 m

SHOSHONE LAKE
Lewis Lake
Lewis Falls
Lewis River

APPROXIMATE CALDERA BOUNDARY

Eagle Pass
Eagle Peak 11358 ft 3462 m
Highest point in the park
Table Mountain 11063 ft 3372 m
Colter Peak 10683 ft 3256 m
Turret Mountain 10995 ft 3351 m
Trail Creek
Yellowstone River
Reservation Peak 10629 ft 3240 m

SHOSHONE NATIONAL FOREST
WASHAKIE WILDERNESS
ABSAROKA RANGE

MADISON PLATEAU
CASCADE CORNER
Buffalo Lake
PITCHSTONE PLATEAU

IBOU- GHEE NAL REST
CARIBOU-TARGHEE NATIONAL FOREST
IDAHO / MONTANA
MONTANA / IDAHO

CONTENTS

CHAPTER I

UPPER, MIDWAY, LOWER GEYSER BASINS

"Old woman's Grandchild fought many beasts and turned them into mountains and hills after he killed them. A large buffalo bull that he killed was turned into a geyser formation that continued to blow out hot air. Near it he placed a montain lion, also a geyser formation blowing hot air, in order to keep the buffalo bull from coming back to life."

— Crow Narrative

The mystery and story of Yellowstone take place out of sight and deep beneath Earth's surface. From a depth of 1800 miles, and extending to the very center of our planet, around 4000 miles, lies a great furnace producing heat rivaling temperatures on the surface of the Sun. Here we encounter Earth's core, which in the center consists of an iron plasma where temperatures rise well above the 2,800° Fahrenheit melting point of iron and reach as much as 10,800° Fahrenheit. The outer region of the core, consisting primarily of molten iron and nickel, is characterized by convection currents that give rise to the protective magnetic field around Earth.

Above the outer core lies the mantle, an 1800-mile-thick region of silicate rock. The heat from the core causes the mantle to become viscous and leads to gradual convection currents in this rock. In some locations, hotter regions of the outer core melt rock within the lower mantle, resulting in a rising column of hot molten rock within the surrounding cooler mantle. As this column of molten rock continues to rise, it reaches the base of the lithosphere, the region of the upper mantle and crust that make up the continental and oceanic plates. The bottom of the lithosphere is heated, melting into hot molten magma. The region of magma expands radially and rises upward as a dome, which in turn pushes the crust upward and results in enormous magma chambers. When the crust cracks, magma is released in volcanic eruptions. The evacuation of these magma chambers leaves a void beneath the surface resulting in the collapse of unsupported overlying land and the formation of a caldera. Areas such as this where magma rises within the mantle leading to volcanic eruptions are called hot spots. Yellowstone is one such area.

Long ago, dating back around 540 million years ago, the area of Yellowstone lay beneath a vast shallow sea. About 66 million years ago, oceanic plate subduction beneath the North American plate gave rise to the Rocky Mountains. Around 15 million years ago, as the North American plate continued in its migration towards the southwest, it passed over a hot spot in the upper mantle.

The events that gave rise to Yellowstone began 2.1 million years ago when the release of magma resulted in a supervolcano. The explosive blast that resulted released lava, which eventually cooled into columnar basalt, and spread ash as far as Missouri that hardened over time to form the Huckleberry Tuff. This eruption resulted in the Yellowstone Caldera, centered in western Yellowstone.

Around 1.3 million years ago, a second supervolcanic eruption occurred, not as large as its predecessor. This eruption released lava and spread ash as far as central Kansas, resulting in the Mesa Falls Tuff. The Island Park Caldera, overlying the western portion of the Yellowstone Caldera, resulted from this eruption.

Around 640,000 years ago, a third supervolcano erupted, the second largest of the three eruptions. During this eruption, ash spread as far as central Louisiana, ultimately hardening into the Lava Creek Tuff. The Yellowstone II Caldera, within and 10 miles to the east of the Yellowstone Caldera, resulted from this eruption. Yellowstone Lake lies within the Yellowstone II Caldera.

Around 150,000 years ago, periodic rhyolite (the volcanic equivalent of granite) lava flow appeared within the floor of the Yellowstone II Caldera, giving shape to Yellowstone's lakes, waterfalls, and streams. Upstream from the Lower Yellowstone Falls, water flows over this more resistant rhyolite. However, geothermal activity weakening the rhyolite downstream from these falls likely resulted in the deepening and widening of the Grand Canyon of the Yellowstone as we know it today.

Other mysterious geothermal phenomena occur within the Yellowstone Caldera, including significant geyser activity. There are also less dynamic thermal features such as fumaroles, hot springs, and mud pots. When it rains or snowfall melts, water finds its way into cracks and fissures in the ground. When this cold water comes into contact with shallow magma chambers, it is heated beyond its boiling point to as much as 400° Fahrenheit. This superheated water then works its way upwards through the cracks and fissures and, depending on the amount of water and extent of heat, manifests at the surface as geysers or smaller thermal features. Hot springs form when the superheated water moves upwards slowly with the gradual release of pressure. If the movement of the water is restricted, the release is more explosive in the form of geysers. If the amount of water is limited, or much of it evaporates before reaching the surface, fumaroles, or small releases of steam, result. If the water is not quite so hot but is acidic, it dissolves the surrounding rocks at the surface resulting in mud pots of silica and clay.

OLD FAITHFUL

OLD FAITHFUL

EXCELSIOR GEYSER

CALOTHRIX, SYNECHOCOCCUS, AND PHORMIDIUM BACTERIA

GRAND PRISMATIC SPRING

CHAPTER 2
NORRIS GEYSER BASIN AND ARTISTS PAINTPOT

"The wildest geysers in the world, in bright, triumphant bands, are dancing and singing in it amid thousands of boiling springs, beautiful and awful, their basins arrayed in gorgeous colors like gigantic flowers; and hot paint-pots, mud springs, mud volcanoes, mush and broth caldrons whose contents are of every color and consistency, plashing, heaving, roaring, in bewildering abundance."
— JOHN MUIR

Somewhere in the universe, there is a young planet still cooling from its primordial molten state and where conditions are extreme. High temperatures and acidity may be prevalent such that we postulate that life could not exist under such conditions. Earth, however, presents evidence that not only can life survive in extreme environments, but that it can thrive. Archaea, single-celled organisms absent a nucleus, are found thriving in places characterized by such extreme conditions. Archaea, derived from "archae", meaning ancient, are thought to be descendants of some of the first forms of life and that similarly resided in the extreme young Earth environment.

One such place on where life prevails in the extreme is Yellowstone National Park. High temperature, extreme pH, highly mineralized water emerges from beneath the surface resulting in thermal features such as geysers, hot springs, and their associated runoff. And yet archaea, bacteria, and eukarya (single or multi-celled organisms with a nucleus) are bountiful in long filaments or thick mats. Microorganisms living under these conditions are called thermophiles, hyperthermophiles, or extremophiles. Moreover, each of these microbes inhabits a niche environment that varies by temperature, mineral content, or levels of acidity or alkalinity.

Temperature, more than other factors, determines which microbe will be present, and the varying microbes express very distinctive colors. As such, color serves as a living thermometer that can indicate the relative temperature of the water, although mineralogy also sometimes contributes to the color observed.

Norris Geyser Basin is one of the oldest thermal areas characterized by some of the highest temperatures and predominantly highly acidic waters associated with multiple geysers. For example, in the Pinwheel Geyser, water temperatures are 109°F (43°C), and the acidity of 3.42 matches that of vinegar. Never-the-less, one of the most heat- and acid-tolerant algae known makes its home here - a red alga called Cyanidioschyzon. This organism derives its energy from photosynthesis and grows to form lime green (from chlorophyll) mats over the orange-red iron deposits in the runoff from this geyser.

In contrast, the Whirligig Geyser exhibits much higher temperatures than other nearby geysers and is highly acidic with a pH of 3.4. These extreme conditions limit the microorganisms able to reside in these waters.

Metallosphaera, considered a hyperthermophile and capable of thriving in temperatures up to 176°F (80°C), is an Archaea that thrives here. Metallosphaera can dissolve metals and derives its energy from the oxidation of iron and sulfur in the water. This alga forms an orange microbial community, which along with iron oxides and arsenic, gives rise to the bright orange colors in runoff from this geyser.

In the Constant Geyser, water temperatures are 100°F (38°C) with water characterized by high acidity with a pH of 3.46. The slightly cooler water as compared with other geysers gives rise to other microorganisms that reside here such as Zygogonium, a photosynthetic green alga. Zygogonium form thick mats that provide habitat for microorganisms. Under intense sunlight, these algae release a purple pigment giving the mats a dark purple or black color.

Midway Geyser Basin of Yellowstone boasts the Grand Prismatic Spring with a spectrum of color reflecting the mineralogy and microorganisms present. This hot spring spans 370 feet across and reaches a depth of 121 feet. Extreme water temperatures range from 145°F to 188°F (63°C to 87°C), and the high alkalinity (pH of 8.3) matches that of baking soda. The blue water in the central area of the spring is too hot for microorganisms, with its color arising from the reflectivity of water and the presence of dissolved silica.

The thermophile Synechocuccus makes its home around the perimeter of this spring. Synechococcus is a greenish photosynthetic bacterium that thrives in water temperatures up to 165°F (74°C) and neutral to slightly alkaline conditions. These bacteria form green mats. Synechococcus derive energy from photosynthesis and fermentation during the daytime and nighttime, respectively.

Another resident is Phormidium, an orange cyanobacterium that uses sunlight for energy and thrives in temperatures ranging from 95°F to 135°F (35°C to 57°C). These bacteria form mats and may be present in long streamers or as stromatolites (layered structures). NASA may look for evidence of Phormidium on other planets in that it serves as a biomarker for extinct hot springs.

Another resident, Calothrix, makes its home around the perimeter where the water temperature is above 86°F (30°C). They derive energy both from photosynthesis and from fermentation during the daytime and nighttime, respectively. Calothrix is visible in dark brown mats along the moist edges and in the outflow of the spring. They are thought to be the ancestor of early Earth cyanobacteria.

PORCELAIN BASIN

PORCELAIN BASIN

ZYGOGONIUM ALGA AND IRON
OXIDES

CYANIDIOSCHYZON ALGAE

EAST FORK TANTALUS CREEK

METALLOSPHAERA ARCHAEA, IRON OXIDES AND ARSENIC

CYANIDIOSCHYZON ALGAE

METALLOSPHAERA ARCHAEA

LEDGE GEYSER / BLACK GROWLER STEAM VENT

EMERALD SPRING

STEAMBOAT GEYSER

CISTERN SPRING

ARTISTS PAINTPOT

ARTISTS PAINTPOT

ARTISTS PAINTPOT

CHAPTER 3

MAMMOTH HOT SPRINGS

"Everybody needs beauty as well as bread, places to play in and pray in, where nature may heal and give strength to body and soul."
— John Muir

Located in the northern portion of Yellowstone, Mammoth Hot Springs is a work of art crafted by nature over time. The springs display intricate terraces resembling the landscape of a distant planet. Although outside of the Yellowstone Caldera, the springs result from the same geothermal phenomenon that led to thermal features elsewhere in the park. As snowmelt or precipitation find its way into the subsurface through cracks and fissures, the water becomes quickly superheated by magma chambers associated with historic volcanic activity. The hot water observed at Mammoth Hot Springs is understood to originate in Norris, where it flows along a fault line toward Mammoth. The superheated water then works its way back upward through the network of fissures while also interacting with gases rising from the magma. As a result, carbon dioxide dissolves into the hot water lowering its acidity. As this acidic water works its way toward the surface, it passes through and dissolves limestone. When the superheated water reaches the surface, carbon dioxide is lost to the air, and dissolved limestone deposits as a white chalky mineral called travertine. These deposits of travertine result in the intricate terraces observed in Mammoth Hot Springs.

These hot springs are also home to a diverse population of microorganisms that thrive in its hot but only slightly acidic to alkaline waters. The Orange Spring mound is home to green bacteria such as Chloroflexus and Chlorobium that thrive in the roughly neutral pH water of the spring at around 113°F (45°C). These bacteria mix with cyanobacteria creating mats that vary in color from dark green in the winter to light green-yellow in summer in response to the prevalence or absence of sunlight.

The hot springs are also home to orange photosynthetic cyanobacteria, Oscillatoria. Their name derives from their motion in response to light. The bacteria and algae form mats that are home to predatory microbes, protozoa called Chilodonella, that feast on the bacteria and algae.

Mammoth Springs also hosts bacteria such as Thermochromatium, which derive energy from the oxidation of sulfur and form deep purple or reddish-brown mats.

Another microorganism that makes its home in Mammoth Hot Springs is Sulfurihydrogenibium. These bacteria reside in areas where temperatures range from 140°F to 167°F (60°C to 75°C) in roughly neutral pH water. They derive energy from the mineralogy in the water, oxidizing sulfur, iron, or hydrogen. Sulfurihydrogenibium is visible as cream filaments or streamers.

———◦◦———

After becoming a national park in 1872, Mammoth Hot Springs became the administrative headquarters under civilian control. Tourism to the park increased. The U.S. government was relocating Native Americans to reservations at this time, which, in part, contributed to the eventual transfer of control of Yellowstone to the military. Of particular note was the flight of the Nez Perce in the summer of 1877. The U.S. Army was under orders to move the Nez Perce tribe to a reservation. Following the killing of several Idaho settlers by young warriors and increased pressure, the Nez Perce led their people away with the intent of a peaceful migration to Canada. However, their journey entailed frequent skirmishes with the Army and the death of several tourists. On August 25, 1877, a group of tourists camping in the vicinity of Mammoth Hot Springs sighted the passing Nez Perce to the south. Warriers entered their camp the next day and the tourists were scattered, except Charles Kenck who was killed. Several, including Richard Dietrich, found their way back to Mammoth Hot Springs. On August 27 some went to look for men who had not made it back. Several skirmishes with the Nez Perce occured over the following days and Dietrich was killed. The remainder of the tourists made it out. Although the Nez Perce made it out of Yellowstone, the Army stopped them within 40 miles from the Canadian border.

After fourteen years of civilian control, the Calvary took over the administration, including the management of tourism and natural resources, in 1886. The Calvary built a temporary post near Mammoth Hot Springs. However, after several harsh winters and the realization that their stewardship would not be temporary, the Army began Fort Yellowstone construction in 1891. The first clapboard buildings were constructed, including a guardhouse. President Theodore Roosevelt visited the park in 1903 and placed the cornerstone in Roosevelt Arch that marks the entrance to Yellowstone National Park just north of Mammoth Hot Springs. Fort Yellowstone was completed in 1909 with the construction of stone buildings to increase the capacity to 400 men. Then in 1916, the National Park Service was formed with control over Yellowstone returning to civilians.

PALETTE SPRING

CHLOROFLEXUS, CHLOROBIUM, AND OSCILLATORIA BACTERIA

PALETTE SPRING

ANGEL TERRACE

THERMOCHROMATIUM BACTERIA

ELK

PRONGHORN

CHAPTER 4

HAYDEN VALLEY

"...that no white man should ever be told of this inferno, lest he should enter that [Yellowstone] region and form a league with the devils, and by their aid come forth and destroy all Indians.

— John Hamilcar Hollister

There are undoubtedly countless tales that would convey the history of Native Americans in Yellowstone. However, it seems that such stories were not forthcoming to Euro-American fur traders who ventured into the area in the late 18th century. Instead, Euro-Americans, hoping to increase interest in the area, and establish that it was safe to visit, spread a false narrative that suggested Indians were afraid of Yellowstone and its enigmatic thermal features. More likely, Yellowstone was sacred to many tribes who would have been understandably reluctant to invite inquiry into the area. Their reluctance to speak of Yellowstone has remained a mystery. However, the reason for their silence has become clear from a rare book found in the private library of a Montana resident. This book was published in 1912 by John Hollister that had traveled to the area in 1883. John Hollister wrote that the Indians feared that upon discovering Yellowstone, whites would conspire with devils and that this would lead to the destruction of all Indians. To the extent that Euro-Americans migrating into the area sought to displace Indians and exploit Yellowstone, such as through tourism, their fear was not baseless.

While stories were not forthcoming, archeological evidence such as the discovery of ancient campsites and trails does provide insight into the history of Native Americans and their ancestors in the area. Furthermore, the evidence suggests that the Paleoindians -- ancient ancestors of Native Americans – migrated into the area sometime following the end of the last major ice age that ended around 11,700 years ago. At least 1,850 archaeological sites provide evidence that Paleoindians and more recent Native American ancestors visited or inhabited the area from about 11,000 to 1,000 years ago. Ancient artifacts discovered at these sites include stone tools and stone weapons known as Clovis points or Folsom points – knife blades or spear points fashioned from obsidian found in Yellowstone. One Folsom point is estimated to date back 10,900 years. Others found around Yellowstone Lake have been dated to 9,350 years. Additional evidence suggests the evolution of weaponry from throwing spears, or atlatl, to the bow and arrow. Due to the high elevation, averaging 8,000 feet above sea level, Native American ancestors would likely have traveled seasonally to or through Yel-

lowstone to hunt bison or bighorn sheep. They also traveled to Yellowstone to obtain obsidian or for ceremonial or medicinal purposes. These early migrants experienced the "Burning Mountains" before the first roads and before the onset of tourism. The enigmatic wilderness would have inspired thoughts of the supernatural and awareness of powers and spirits beyond their understanding.

Moreover, oral histories suggest the use or occasional inhabitance of the Yellowstone territory by various tribes. Oral histories place the Salish people in the region as much as 3,000 years ago. Euro-Americans sometimes referred to the Salish as Flatheads due to their practice of artificial cranial deformation. From 1300 and 1700, oral histories place tribes such as the Shoshone, Kiowa, Crow, and Sioux in Yellowstone. As Euro-Americans ventured into the area during the 19th century, four tribes lived in proximity to Yellowstone, including Crow to the east, Shoshone and Bannock to the west, and Blackfeet hunting on the plains to the west and south.

Kiowa People

Native Americans and their ancestors depended on bison for meat and used the fur and hide for clothing, blankets, and to cover their tipis. Hunting presumably with the atlatl, and later the bow and arrow, the harvesting of bison was sustainable with herds estimated to have numbered 30 to 60 million during the 1500s. Pressure on bison populations increased around 1820 when Native Americans, driven from their lands in the east, brought horses and guns. Bison populations declined almost to extinction beginning around 1830 as Euro-Americans migrated to the area and killed them by the hundreds of thousands as a strategy to conquer Native Americans. An industry motivated by greed and characterized by indifference to the decimated bison herds dramatically decreased populations. The market for bison hides increased. The bones ground up provided fertilizer for farmlands in the Great Plains. States passed laws to protect bison. However, without enforcement, bison populations continued to decline. By 1902, bison in Yellowstone numbered only about 23. In 1905, the American Bison Society formed to protect and restore bison herds, with Theodore Roosevelt as honorary president. As of August 2019, the bison herd in Yellowstone numbered 4,829. This herd is allowed to roam freely over Yellowstone and parts of Montana.

BISON HERD

BLACK WOLF

CHAPTER 5

YELLOWSTONE RIVER

"At the head of this river the natives give an account that there is frequently herd a loud noise, like thunder, which makes the earth tremble, they state that they seldom go there because their children cannot sleep – and conceive it possessed of spirits, who were averse that men should [be] near them."
— William Clark, 1804-1806 Expedition

The path for Yellowstone to become a national park was driven initially by stories from fur trappers and others who traveled to the area, but their stories were not initially taken seriously. With time more serious expeditions ventured to the area and the need to preserve the area became clear.

With the 1803 Louisiana purchase from France, the path was clear for exploration into the unknown west. Under direction from President Thomas Jefferson, Lewis and Clark led an expedition from 1804 to 1806 up the Missouri River to search for a water passage to the Pacific Ocean. The party passed north of Yellowstone, and despite accounts from Native Americans, did not travel south to explore the region. However, on their return journey from the Pacific Coast in 1806, one of their scouts, John Colter, chose to remain in the Rockies rather than return home. In the winter of 1807, and under the employ of Spanish trader Manual Lisa, John Colter traveled into the Yellowstone region. His instruction was to establish fur trading relations with Indians. On this journey, he encountered the Crow and joined them on a hunting expedition during which they came across a hostile band of Blackfeet. During the ensuing battle, Colter fought on the side of the victorious Crow.

This incident perhaps paved the way for amicable relations with the Crow over the ensuing decades of fur trading and settlement. It may have also established hostile relations with Blackfeet that later developed a reputation for taking potshots and killing numerous white settlers.

The fur trade in the Yellowstone region accelerated in 1818 as trappers ventured into this relatively unknown territory. Philetus Norris, the later Superintendent of Yellowstone National Park, discovered a carving in a pine tree. The carving read "J.O.R., Aug 29, 1819". Norris never uncovered the identity of the likely trapper who made the engraving. In 1829, a party of American fur trappers approached Yellowstone from the north. A Blackfoot war party attacked the traders who scattered in their retreat. A 19-year-old named Joseph Meek escaped across the Yellowstone River with his mule, blanket, and gun. In his escape, Meek later wrote

that he came into an area where "the whole country beyond was smoking with the vapor from boiling springs and burning with gasses, issuing from small craters".

"I have been told the sun would be blown out, and the earth burn up. If this infernal wind keeps up, I shouldn't be surprised if the sun war blown out. If the earth is not burning up over thar, then it is that place the old Methodist preacher used to threaten me with."
— Joseph L. Meek, 1829

Early stories of Yellowstone were embellished and fanciful. Consequently, readers of later accounts were skeptical. More serious expeditions began with the Folsum Party expedition, led by David Folsom, in 1869. Publicists viewed their account skeptically though it was ultimately published, albeit with manuscript pieces cut out, by the Western Monthly Magazine.

A subsequent 1870 expedition into Yellowstone occurred and was led by General Washburn. Notably, Lieutenant Doane reported the account of this expedition as a Government document. His report reached the attention of U.S. Representative William Kelley in 1871. Representative Kelley later advanced the notion of establishing Yellowstone as a national park.

A third expedition followed in 1871, led by the then Secretary of Interior Ferdinand Hayden. This expedition was scientific and intended to gather information on the geology, mineralogy, zoology, botany, and agricultural resources associated with Yellowstone. Captain John W. Barlow, the chief engineer of the Army Division of Missouri, accompanied the expedition that became known as the Haydon Barlow Party. Notably, Philadelphia artist Thomas Moran also joined the party and produced perhaps the first sketches and paintings of Yellowstone sharing its beauty with the public back east. Before their return, the party observed settlers and cabins in the vicinity of Yellowstone.

A letter from A.B. Nettleton, written on stationery from the Northern Pacific Railroad Company, was sent to Ferdinand Hayden, then in Washington D.C., suggesting that Yellowstone be reserved for public use rather than give way to private development. The letter precipitated a series of events that culminated in the establishment of Yellowstone National Park. On March 1, 1872, President Ulysses S Grant signed the law establishing Yellowstone National Park "for the benefit and enjoyment of the people."

LOWER FALLS

GRAND CANYON OF
THE YELLOWSTONE

YELLOWSTONE RIVER

CRYSTAL FALLS

UPPER FALLS

www.ingramcontent.com/pod-product-compliance
Lightning Source LLC
Chambersburg PA
CBHW042108090426

42811CB00018B/1888